First... Then...

Also by Melinda Smith and published by Ginninderra Press
Pushing thirty, wearing seventeen
Mapless in Underland

Melinda Smith

First... Then...

poems from planet autism

Supported by

First… Then…: poems from planet autism
ISBN 978 1 74027 734 1
Copyright © Melinda Smith 2012

First published 2012
Reprinted 2015

GINNINDERRA PRESS
PO Box 3461 Port Adelaide SA 5015
www.ginninderrapress.com.au

Contents

Foreword	7
First…then…	9
Brain Weather	13
Autistic Acrostic	14
Beach cricket with four-year-old	15
autistic child with acute auditory processing disorder	16
what the child hears	18
I prefer	19
What I learned at school	20
Asperger's diagnosis: a fugue	21
Not the Botany Bay song	23
A prehistory of autism	24
On holding the baby of a friend	26
But	27
Social Stories for Neurotypical Adults #27: No Dogs Allowed	28
All magpies are autistic	30
The impossible blindfold	32
Love song of autistic husband	33
An autistic woman explains the terror of affection	35
Shechinah – or God and Temple Grandin	37
AUTISM CRUMPETS	39
I have autism	40
I am autistic	44
AutisTweets	45
#autismtshirtslogans	47

Foreword

I have never written a foreword for a book of poems before. However, this is a very special kind of book and I think it deserves a few words to accompany it on its journey out into the world.

All of the poems in this book are about life with autism. Most of them are what is called in the trade 'dramatic monologues' – that is, they are written in the voice of a character. Some of the voices belong to autistic adults, some to autistic children, some to parents, carers and siblings of autistic people.

Obviously, as I am the parent of a child with autism, many of the poems are informed by my experiences, those of my son, and those of other family members. However, this is not an autobiography or a biography. It is one set of creative responses to a journey which many people happen to find themselves on. I have published these poems so that others on that journey can read them and know they are not alone, and so that their friends and relatives, and the general reader, can perhaps have a tiny peek into a world which is often misunderstood, misrepresented or ignored. I do not claim these poems to be the last (or the first) word on life with autism, just one set of sketches out of millions of possible ones.

In presuming, in some of the following poems, to write in the voice of a person with autism when I myself am not autistic, I am aware that I may be open to criticism from some in the self-advocacy movement. Surely I should get out of the way and let autistic people speak for themselves? In reply, all I can say is that I am not preventing anyone from telling their own story, I am merely engaging in the time-honoured creative practice of standing in the shoes of my fellow humans in the hope that we may all start to better understand each other.

Furthermore, in most cases I have framed my 'autistic voice' poems as responses to first-hand accounts written by autistic people, thus (I hope) furthering the efforts those people have already made to tell their own stories.

Thank you to ArtsACT and the ACT Government for the New Projects Grant I received in 2011. This allowed me one day a week over twelve months to write, revise and publicise (via Facebook, Twitter (@MelindaLSmith) and my blog www.circlequirk.wordpress.com) most of the poems in this collection.

I also owe a large debt of gratitude to the following people and organisations:

- Glenn Colquhoun, without whose initial encouragement this book might still be stuck inside me;
- Stephen Matthews, for publishing my previous books and for promptly expressing his support for this one, enabling me to lodge the grant application on time;
- Suzanne Edgar, Martin Dolan and Michael Thorley for their camaraderie, encouragement and fearlessness with the blue pencil;
- Les Murray and George Thomas of *Quadrant* magazine for publishing earlier forms of some of these poems, and for their support and encouragement;
- *Blackmail Press*, *ACT Carers' Circle*, Vagabond Press's *Geek Mook* and the websites of Dr Tony Attwood, Scottish Autism and Aspie in the Family for publishing / posting earlier versions of some of these poems;
- the autism communities on Twitter and Facebook for embracing earlier versions of these poems and sharing them so widely with each other; and
- my wonderful partner Michael and our two sons, without whom none of it would have been possible.

First...then...

First change nappy
Then Thomas the Tank Engine

First clothes on
Then sandpit

First wash hair
Then chocolate frog

First the only baby crying all night in the hospital
> Then the only baby wailing for the whole of mothers' group

First the only mother convinced her child was permanently angry
> Then the only one holding him in her arms and doing deep knee bends to calm him down

First thinking it was normal to scream until throwing up whenever we changed routine
> Then shocked when I realised other families didn't have to live like that

First astonished he could read at eighteen months
> Then astonished at his shrieks every time his baby brother cried

First proud of every fact he could recite about the planet Jupiter
> Then wondering why he needed twelve weeks of physio to learn how to jump

First hair cut
Then play with spray bottle

First stop biting Mummy
Then play with sliding door

First poo *in toilet*
Then flush

First letting his father talk me out of it
    Then talking myself out of it
First knowing those therapists just didn't get my child
    Then googling autism with a chill in my heart
First joking about 'our little Rain Man'
    Then realising the joke was on me

First paralysis
    Then fear
First incomprehension
    Then overload

First Music Therapy
    Then Homeopathy
First Triple-P Parenting for Parents of Children with
    Disabilities
    Then Encouraging the Reluctant Eater
First Occupational Therapy
    Then the social worker
First trusting the system
    Then realising the system didn't care enough or have
    enough money

First sit at table to eat
Then spinning with Mummy

First swallow medicine
Then build washing machine from cardboard boxes

First reading lots of parent testimonials
> Then feeling like scum for not doing six hours of therapy with him every day

First wonderfully affirmed by *Welcome to Holland*
> Then convinced *Welcome to Holland* left a lot of shit out

First talking to happy well-adjusted mums of older kids on the spectrum
> Then terrified our family would disintegrate before our kids ever got to that age

First poring over *Autism and Asperger's Syndrome for those who love and care for three-to-seven-year-olds*
> Then realising the only book I needed to read was *The Curious Incident of the Dog in the Night Time*

First joining support groups
> Then walking out of meetings because the horror stories people told at them could not possibly be true

First counselling
> Then drugs

First sobbing to my friends
> Then avoiding my friends and hating their normal uncomplicated children

First hearing that carers of autistic children are as stressed as soldiers in combat
> Then bawling my eyes out

First thread beads on string
Then letterbox-counting walk

First stay at special needs soccer for ten minutes
Then computer time

First nearly destroying my marriage
    Then clinging to my marriage
First regretting the second child
    Then realising the second child would probably save us all
First wanting my husband to see things my way
    Then grateful he didn't
First mourning my old life
    Then understanding you never really get it back anyway
First obsessed with getting the whole family to accept the diagnosis
    Then learning to take what help I could get and live with the elephant in the room

First shame
    Then resentment
First desperate for pity
    Then desperate for respite care
First whining
    Then laughing

First crawling through it
    Then writing about it
First today
    Then tomorrow

Brain Weather

autistic meltdown ground zero

Think of   hemispheres: Western, Left;
the wind-flows   that connect them; the currents
    of sea; of electricity.

When was it that   your frontal   lobe
Cauterised   itself against your   will
leaving you endless   atomised local   storms
with no way   to blow them   -selves out?

The last words you   said before the clouds came
stutter on   your small   tongue;
settle   in like cat-and   -dog rain, the syllables
hammering down, fixing one   thought with   a dozen
    stabs of lightning.
The miracle is not that it   stops, but how afterwards
    you can be so   calm and charming
– and puzzled that the rest of us still   drip and shiver
    from the rain.

Autistic Acrostic

Any day now, it will lift.
Under your mask of howls, I see
Two knowing eyes reproaching me,
Incensed that I should try to shift
Some blame, for this, our hell, to you.
Mummy feels like howling too.

Beach cricket with four-year-old

Bat and ball
glow brightest summer yellow.
Mango-yellow; floatie-yellow; *Slip'n'Slide* yellow.
He loses patience
with hit and miss; prefers
to float them both –
mismatched vessels –
in the long flat lace-wash close to shore.
The water loves its new toys,
drags and tumbles them
never quite letting go.
He studies the shallows, points
at a bubble cluster.
'A galaxy! A galaxy!'
And suddenly the hollow
plastic things are flotsam
adrift on space-time;
an oblong and a sphere,
still loud yellow.
Rocket-flame-yellow; sun-yellow.

autistic child with acute auditory processing disorder

in the foetal position in the museum toilets,
hands clamped over my ears, shrieking
trying to say *there's a dryer, there's a dryer*, any second now
someone will set it off
the sound will be a faceful of boiling water

> I'm sorry, your patient
> explanations are not getting
> through. It's a very bad line.

at the indoor swimming pool, crouched behind the waterslide,
poo-ing into my damp trunks
trying to say *I have to get out*, the echoes
are attacking me in four dimensions, I'm on a bad trip
and I can't come down

at the washing line, moaning
trying to burrow under the grass
trying to say *there's a bird, there's a bird*, it's going to swoop down
it's going screech in my ear
the sound will ice-pick my skull

> Your cognitive behaviour
> therapy is not getting through at
> all. It *is* a very bad line.

at a birthday party, buried under cushions and wailing like a siren
trying to say *I can't stand it*, the music and the voices
are tearing at me, pecking me apart

in my bedroom after school, kicking my baby sister in the face
trying to say *go away, go away*, you're noisy, you're unpredictable
I've been clinging to a cliff face for six hours
and you're dangling yourself from my ankles

sprinting straight into traffic, terrified
of a toy poodle on the footpath
trying to say *there's a dog, there's a dog*, it's going to bark
the sound will slug me like a sandpaper boxing glove

> Your elaborate reward and
> punishment system, your
> guilt trips, your lectures, your
> bellowing and tears aren't
> getting through either. This is a
> *very* bad line.

what the child hears

the sheep are speaking
to the frogs who are speaking
to the ravens who are speaking
to the crickets who are speaking
to the horses who are speaking
to the flies who are speaking
to the trucks on the highway who are speaking
to the ripples in the water who are speaking
to the farm dog who is speaking
to the metal bucket who is speaking
to the dragonfly who is speaking
to the plane who is speaking
to the reeds who are speaking
to the tractor who is speaking
to the mosquitoes who are speaking
to the magpies who are speaking
to the chainsaw who is speaking
to the sulphur-crested cockatoos who are speaking
to the farmer's wife who is speaking
to the chickens who are speaking
to the frogs who are speaking
to the sheep who are speaking
to me

I prefer

serious illness to surprises
computers to my brother
reading number plates to Christmas morning

straight lines
submerging my ears in a warm bath to waterslides
deep fat fryers to matchbox cars

torture to haircuts
libraries to birthday parties
standing ankle-deep in ocean

tenpin bowling to climbing trees
looking at things out of the corner of my eye
Sonic the Hedgehog to family time

death to dentist visits
my mother with her glasses off
plastic wheelie bins to petting zoos

not to see my school friends outside of school
cricket statistics to *Toy Story*
chewing clothes-pegs to talking

rules to freedom
truth to sarcasm
home

to be left alone

What I learned at school

Again today he said he was my friend.
He made me spin around till I was sick.
So is that bullying, or just pretend?

I said my money was for *me* to spend.
He told Miss Green I hit him with a brick.
Again today he says he is my friend.

The others, when they see him coming, send
him straight to where I am. He's pretty quick.
So is that bullying, or just pretend?

He took me to the toilet down the end
and wet the urinal and made me lick.
Again today he said he was my friend,

but after that he made me stand, and bend,
then poked me in the bottom with a stick.
So is that bullying, or just pretend?

My teacher told me off: *'This has to end.*
By now you should have wised up to this trick.'
Again today he says he is my friend.
So is that bullying, or just pretend?

Asperger's diagnosis: a fugue

The cup finishes. I see. I look and look and hold on to it. It
  makes sense now. Cup. Hand. It *finishes*.
In *my* football draw there will be no elimination matches
I don't have Asperger's syndrome. I was terrified the horses and
  cows would fall off the hill
Here comes the Schumaker-Levy 9! Here it comes!
We called for hours and hours, why didn't you answer?
I was being under a pyramid

The cup *finishes*. It makes sense now. I don't have Asperger's
  syndrome
David says I do but he's wrong.
In *my* football draw the only elimination match will be the final
If there were no gravity we would all float up into the air and the
  oceans would leak away into space
We called for hours and hours, why didn't you answer?
I dreamed there was a big chicken in my room trying to eat my legs

I don't have Asperger's syndrome. I look and look and hold onto
it.
You say I do but you're wrong. In Me-land money, the notes start
  at seven cruzlaks
Elimination matches are REALLY unfair
Roman baths were a lot like our health clubs
We called for hours and hours, why didn't you answer?
I was terrified the horses and cows would fall

Cup. Hand. Cup. Hand. Asperger's syndrome is dumb.
I don't think there should be any more elimination matches,
 ever. I don't
The doctor says I do but he's a baddie!
The notes start at seven cruzlaks because there is a five-
 cruzlak coin
We called for hours and hours, why didn't you answer?
The elephant bird was the biggest bird that ever lived

We called for hours and hours, why didn't you answer?
I knew where you were.

Parts of this poem are a poetic response to the book *Smiling at Shadows*, Junee Waites & Helen Swinbourne, HarperCollins 2001.

Not the Botany Bay song

A sea shanty for ASD parents and carers

Ohhh…
Farewell to the high life forever
Farewell to my suits and my heels
For my child's on the autism spectrum:
my career juggernaut's lost its wheels.

Singing echo-lay, echo-lay, la-li-a
Singing meltdowns as public disgrace
Singing though we might live in Australia
It can seem we've been shot into space.

Well our home is all plastered with visuals
and we never have guests as a rule
and the unstructured horror of holidays
means we can't wait to get back to school.

Singing maybe this thing is contagious
Singing I used to think I was fine
But now all of my best friends are therapists
– or they're parents of children like mine.

Then there's friendships and hygiene and puberty
and employment and learning to lie.
It's a long row to hoe, that's for certain sure
– and then who'll step in when you die?

Singing once I was witty and erudite
Singing once I had beauty to spare
Now I bang on about intervention plans
and I think I've got lice in my hair.

> '[T]he first stone spear…was probably invented by an Aspie who chipped away at rocks while the other people socialized around the campfire.'
> – Temple Grandin

A prehistory of autism

This one can run and run, never tiring;
climb trees and cliffs until the gibbons are afraid for him.
Even when he falls he feels no pain. He has little need of sleep.
He speaks only by repeating what he hears
but he is the best of night watchmen
and in the hunt he is magnificent.

That one scents the lions on the wind;
smells the poison in the berries.
If her special stone is taken away
she makes wounded beast howls
but she can spot a snake's hole at forty paces
from three newly bent twigs and a fresh hollow in the dust.

This other knows the places of the stars by heart.
He speaks often of the wandering ones:
he can see their journeys as clear as the track to the waterhole
although he will not look any man in the eye.
He sits alone all day, dotting sky pictures on pieces of bark.
Only he knows the day when the wildebeest will move.

That one over there has no love but for making spears.
He chips stone after stone until the sun is low;
walks far to find strong wood for the shafts.
He does not join the hunt: he is slow and clumsy
and does not do what he is told – but in the hands of others
his weapons fly true and bring down many of the herd.

Another has the gift of singing –
all melodies are hers at one hearing.
She has mastered the speech of those over the mountain
and of the fishers by the lake.
She will not let men come to her, although she is grown.
She screams and spits at any who try. Her kind smiles are
    only for small children
and for those who bring her new songs.

On holding the baby of a friend

I hug and nuzzle; brush my cheek to his.
He giggles, grabs my nose and grins at me.
I close my eyes and pray no one will see
the tear I shed at how much fun this is.
I'm sprung: '*Clucky again? Another son?*'
How can I tell her so she'll understand?
I had so much of this to give: I planned
to shower it all on mine. He wanted none.

I wonder whether mothers get a store
of child-affection, swelling in the chest
like milk come in, demanding to be used.
Does having to suppress it make you sore?
MyWebMD has nothing to suggest.
I borrow babies. They reduce the bruise.

But

When I asked him about his favourite game *DeathBattle 5000*,
I said 'level' instead of 'round'.
He kicked me in the shins.
Mum kicked us both off the computer.
After dinner he patted my nose and smiled.
Love my brother. Sometimes he gets angry, but.

I wanted us all to go to Mark's house to play with his trains.
My brother lay on the floor and screamed 'I HAAAATE
MAAARRRK!' (Mark is *his* friend).
Mum said I would have to go with her another time.
Before bed, he read me a *Captain Underpants* story.
Love my brother. Sometimes he gets angry, but.

I wanted to have my party at Crazy Monkeys Play Centre.
Mum started writing the invitations.
He tried to tear them up and punched me in the tummy.
'I'm NEVER going to Crazy Monkeys. EVER. AGAIN !!!'
(We were there last week. He went down the giant slide
twenty-four times.)
Mum said I can still have my party there.
Dad will stay home and look after him.

At bath time my brother gave me a squashy hug.
He said I was his favourite thing.
Love my brother. Sometimes he gets angry, but.

Social Stories for Neurotypical Adults #27: No Dogs Allowed

I love my dog.
My dog's name is Hackles.
I love to go walking with Hackles.
It makes both of us very happy.
Hackles' favourite thing is to run around without her leash on.
I love to see how happy she is when she does this.

There are some places where dogs are not allowed to go.
There are some other places where dogs are allowed,
but only on a leash.
You can tell if you are in one of those places
because there are big signs,
sometimes even with a picture of a dog with a red line through it!
I hate those signs. They make me mad!
I think it is unfair that Hackles can't just go wherever she wants.
Sometimes I just ignore those nasty old signs.

Not everyone loves dogs.
Some people are scared of dogs.
Some children are so scared of dogs they have to scream
and run away
whenever they see a dog.

When someone acts afraid of Hackles, I get really upset.
Hackles is really sweet and wouldn't hurt anyone.
Sometimes I want to take Hackles right up to the scared child
and make them pat her,
just so they can see there is no reason to be afraid.

If I take Hackles too close to a scared child
it could be really dangerous.
The child might run away onto a busy road or into deep water.
Or they might scream so much
that Hackles gets scared and angry and bites them.
Or they might get so upset
they hurt themselves or other people, or me or Hackles.
I do not want this to happen.

I will try to remember
that not everyone loves dogs as much as I do.
I will try to remember
that the 'no dogs allowed' and 'no dogs off leash' areas are there for a reason.
The people and children who are scared of dogs
need to have somewhere they can feel safe.

I will try to remember to do what the signs say.
Smart grown-ups obey signs.

All magpies are autistic

odd body postures and limb movements, such as twisting or flapping

> flutter-flutter. puff. flap-flap. stand. stalk. stop. hoppy – hoppy – hop. stop. waddle-potter. waddle-potter. stop. step. step. step. head on one side. stalk. stalk. stop.

antisocial behaviour from misinterpreting others' intentions

> **Warning…Warning…Birds swooping! Magpies are nesting in this area. If you come too close, they may attack!**

failure to recognise social concepts such as personal space

> 'Mum! The magpie's trying to stand on my sandwich!'

appetite for substances largely non-nutritive (pica)

> 'Muuuum! Now it's trying to eat the plastic wrap!'

seemingly random outbursts of speech and noise-making

> 'Quardle oodle ardle wardle doodle, the magpies say.'*

extreme absorption in one restricted activity

> stock still. stock still. listen. listen. statue. statue. stock still. stock still. listen. listen. statue. sta – STAB THAT WORM!

frequent self-stimulation by viewing shining, sparkling or rapidly oscillating objects

> pretty pretty alfoil. twinkle. twinkle. crinkle. love to watch. shiny bottle cap. light. light bouncing everywhere. pretty.

transgression of behavioural norms from failure to understand social boundaries

    pretty alfoil. want. take it. take it? take it! SNIP!

*from *The Magpies*, Denis Glover

'For my thoughts are not your thoughts, nor are my ways your ways.'
— Isaiah 55:8

The impossible blindfold

an autistic adult prepares for a day in the workplace

Today again I'll strap on my mask for you;
zip up my ludicrous human suit;

force most of my thoughts into small closed boxes
so that when I speak, you are not made uncomfortable.

When I am not trapped in a room full of chattering
sometimes I can pass for one of your kind.

You few who reach for me with well-meaning thoughts:
even you have no clue how hard this is, nor can you.

If you are sighted and want to try blindness,
bind your eyes for a day, a week — you might come close.

But there are no easy ways to shut down your radar,
lock yourself in my clumsy robot cage

and be. *For my thoughts are not your thoughts,*
   nor are my ways your ways.

This poem and the next one are poetic responses to the book *Discovering My Autism: Apologia Pro Vita Sua (With Apologies to Cardinal Newman)*, Edgar Schneider, Jessica Kingsley Publishers, 1999.

'For my thoughts are not your thoughts, nor are my ways your ways.'
— Isaiah 55:8

Love song of autistic husband

It is pleasant to see you;
when i'm near you i'm happy —
and if ever you leave me
i will think it a pity —

but my love is not your love.
You assume that your feelings
are a halo around you
i could see if i tried to;

that your heart is a mystery
i could solve if i wanted —
but to me it's an organ
and the secrets inside it

are just muscles contracting.
I am always a stranger
understanding you sideways
but i'll always be loyal;

i can't help but be truthful
i remember the housework
and i'm there for the children —
surely these are important?

You insist i'm withholding
all my tenderness from you
but it's not like a river
that i've slyly diverted:

it is more like an absence
like a cave or a sinkhole.
When we fight (so you tell me)
you are harrowed with terror

but my anger is over
when my voice has stopped shouting –
it is you seems to carry
little scars for a lifetime.

When i think of the future
i consider you dying:
what will stretch me to breaking
won't be grief at your going

but the alien business
of the funeral, the lawyers.
My routine will be scrambled
i'll be sick to my stomach

i will shout at the children
i will leave the wake early
and when later i'm solo
i will baulk at your absence

i'll be frightened and angry
– but I don't think i'll cry.

                                          Give, but have something to give.

> No man can want you all.
> Live and learn to live.
> When all the barriers fall
> you are nothing at all.

– *Circle and Square*, Edwin Muir

An autistic woman explains the terror of affection

A rushing of the sea:
your smile is drowning me –
I have to fight to live.
Why can't you let me be?
I feel in negative:
Distress is all you give.

Lost as I have been
I dare not let you in
however loud you call.
I cower in my skin
I curl into a ball.
No man must have me all.

You want to show you care?
You will not reach me there,
that is not where I live.
Just barely touch my hair
– that, I may forgive.
Live, and let me live.

Or give me for my own
a button or a stone –
something smooth and small –
and when I am alone
I'll feel you through this wall.
But when the barriers fall

I cannot meet your eye;
you stab me when you try
to look at me at all.
To let you is to die.
I'll go under, I'll fall –
I'll be nothing at all.

This poem is a poetic response to the book *Nobody Nowhere*, Donna Williams, Jessica Kingsley Publishers, 1998.

'Science without religion is lame. Religion without science is blind.'
– Albert Einstein

Shechinah – or God and Temple Grandin

I find Him first in logic: in the science of snowflakes;
in the patterns silver makes on platinum.

Then entropy terrifies me, *chaos* as *telos*.
Without order, I worry: where can He dwell?

Perhaps if He keeps the gate, shepherding each atom
on its path from heat to cold? In this image I remake my
    religion.

I discover Him also in libraries: my serene heavens of silence
and infinite shelving. My dearest wish is an afterlife of
    browsing,

tasting the bliss of the Great System – the halt and the lame
    reclining
in the silent reading corner; angels bringing them books.

Then: a swim in a dip tank drowns my religion;
organophosphates douse my pillar of flame.

The hangover leaves me without my wonder. I am Dorothy,
    aching for awe,
raising the Wizard's curtain, staring at the little old man.

At long last I find Him in science again, not in order but in the
    mystery
of entangled subatomic particles: their synchronised vibrations

span universes in an instant. He is everywhere at once! And again, after all my seeking
He comes to me where I am: He is with me in the slaughterhouses,

with me in the daily work of death. He blesses my sacred charge:
to ease each animal, calmly, with love, through the blind valley of the shadow.

This poem is a poetic response to the book *Thinking in Pictures: My Life with Autism* (expanded edition), Temple Grandin, Vintage, 2010.

AUTISM CRUMPETS

Static 'me' rumpus.
Imp tutu screams.
Mute. Strums. Pica.
Eat up! Mm! Tics-r-us.
Mute Mac purists.
Um…miscast erupt?

Up came mistrust
(rips Mum acutest).
Impact: muse rust.
Tacit 'summer's up'
captures its Mum.

Sure must impact,
must impact user.

Mum stirs teacup.

I have autism

Google-sculpture 1

Do **i have autism**? high-functioning autism, long periods of time, someone's eyes
I Have Autism – Chapter 1 – YouTube
I have autism and I want you to know
True Life (TV series documentary 1998. **I Have Autism**. Documentary. Your rating: 1 2 3 4 5…
What are signs of **Autism**?, i have two month-old twins and still in the… Your children are too young to worry about autism. It isn't usually picked up until after age two (and two is early, usually more like around age three). At this young of an age…
Autism: I have waited four years to get a kiss from my son. Now he's kissing everybody
I'm not misbehaving, **I have autism**. Please be
    understanding
I don't **have autism**. I am autistic.

How do I know if **I have autism**? What is autism? Autism is a lifelong developmental disability and is part of the autism spectrum. People with…

I Have Autism, my favourite book

I have Autism – Christian Forums Hey. My name is Lauren, I was diagnosed with autism in my toddler years.

It's actually very mild, a lot of people don't even know I have it, but.

MTV's **I have Autism**…try-therapy.com… MTV dares to impress with **'I Have Autism'**. The presentation details the lives of three very inspiring young men who all have differing…

Young I'm Not Misbehaving, **I have Autism** Nicholas Lombardi developed this pin, 'I'm not misbehaving, I have Austism', in a beautiful effort to…

Autism Speaks can go away. **I have autism**. I can speak for myself

Do you think **I have autism**?

Autism Resources Miramichi Inc. – Lending LibraryBOOKS '**I have Autism**' – A Child's First Look at Autism by Pat Crissey1001 Great Ideas for Teaching and…

My baby brother and **I have autism**

'**I have autism.** What's your excuse?' T-shirts poke fun at disability, help educate others, mother says. My son Brandon looks like a typical teenager – until he…

'**I Have Autism**' Child Size awareness bracelet is great for non-verbal kids in case they get separated from you. On sale now at FlagsOnCars.com, you patriotic…

Yes, **I have autism**. Stare if you must. I'm not paying attention to you anyway

Could **i have autism**?

Fishpond Australia, **I Have Autism**… What's That? by Paddy McNally Kate Doherty. Buy Books online:

I have autism. Hear me out.

Special Needs 4 Special Needs **I have Autism** – temporary tattoo – I have Autism temporary tattoo. Featuring hot pink text on a bright green…

I'm not rude, **I have autism**

Do **I have Autism**? – NeuroTalk Support Groups no online test is going to give you even a clue if you have autism of not. The ONLY way you will know is if you talk to a doctor, and go to...

New to group and **I have autism**

Syndrom Puzzle Piece by Medical Alert **I Have Autism** Aspergers Syndrom Puzzle Piece Ribbon 2.25 pin back button-badge. Asthma, peanut allergy, severe food allergies, diabetes, tree nut.

Shop **I Have Autism** Framed Prints. Large selection of unique and funny I Have Autism designs. 100% satisfaction guarantee. Fast shipping

Did **I have autism**? [Archive] – Physics Forums

I was too 'weird' for them, due to the fact that **I have autism**. I just did not know the rules of what you were or were not supposed to do. I would come to a party too...

I have autism spectrum disorder? what does this mean? does it mean... I can't make friends?... Share and Enjoy...

I have autism and I want to work with people who have autism, any...

I have autism and I'm not afraid to use it

I am autistic

Google-sculpture 2

because I cannot be separated from how my brain works
, I'm not a brat
: ask me about my needs
, not just an adult with autism. It is a part of who I am. I was born this way. I would not choose to change that
, I'm not crazy
. I can speak. My voice is different, not weak, and if you listened…
. I'm an adult, with a career, a mortgage, and my first grey hairs. I'm female
. I don't have autism. That's a thing I've been saying forfuckingever. And yet people keep insisting on pointedly saying that…
. I'm apparently what they call 'high-functioning', but I don't like the term very much; the division feels artificial
, and I think in pictures. If the philosophers are correct, I…
, and that's even better!
and proud of it, says Indonesian Oscar Yura Dompas, at the launch of his autobiography, *Autistic Journey*, at QB world Book Plaza
: what's your excuse?

AutisTweets

1

my boy perches on the pool's edge/flapping his wet hands/
people are staring/he sees only me, and grins:/'I caught an
imaginary trout' #ASD

2

#micropoetry #ASDparenting #firsteverjointsleepover Both
sons away tonight/after 7 years/I don't recognise this quiet/
or this calm

3

#autism #newdiagnosis #bewilderment with that one
word/a glass wall traps me/i thump and plead/the doctor
looks away

4

The arrivals board/says my plane has landed/your brother
hugs me/you won't let us go home/the cascading numbers/
are too beautiful #ASD

5

#micropoetry #ASD #autism #anxiety 'I still have a
"drenaline feeling"'/so I walk u down the hall/7 years old &
terrified/of Bugs Bunny

6

#ASD #autism How about this one, madam:/calm to chaos in 60 seconds/looks like a Ferrari/handles like a submarine/ oh and we lost the manual

7

4 years old/you splinter doors with your rage/There are questions I dare not ask now/One starts with the number 14/another with 40 #autism

8

locked out of our new house/I scrabble at flyscreens. You shriek./Note to self: explain #autism to neighbours/before they call the cops

#autismtshirtslogans

I'm not melting down, I'm venting

At least my Chewy Tube doesn't cause lung cancer

So I like to climb things. So what? Higher is better. There are no haters up there

I understand NASCAR racing on a much deeper level than you

Your need for spontaneity is exhausting me

Time for a trampoline break!

School? Hell? Tough choice. At least you get to do fun stuff before they put you in hell

Well? How many digits can *you* recite ϖ to?

If you can read this, you need to gently remind me about personal space

www.ingramcontent.com/pod-product-compliance
Lightning Source LLC
Chambersburg PA
CBHW062206100526
44589CB00014B/1976